London
My
London

Poetry books by Victor Keegan

Crossing the Why
Big Bang
Remember to Forget
Alchemy of Age

London My London

Poems by
Victor Keegan

ShakespearesMonkey

First published in 2017
by Shakespearesmonkey
174 Ashley Gardens
London SW1P 1PD

ISBN 978-0954076252

Cover illustration Christopher Keegan
www.chriskeegan.co.uk

Victor Keegan's main web sites
LondonMyLondon.co.uk
victorkeegan.com

Twitter feeds
@vickeegan
@BritishWino
@LonStreetWalker
@ShakespearesLon

First Edition

With special thanks to my family and to the Daneshill Poetry group (for constant inspiration): to The Amethyst Angel for formatting the book for publication and to A Band Called Quinn for turning some of my past poems into music.

Contents

There's nothing left
apart from
memories
concealed.
Tread softly,
as you would
in any minefield.

Doodlebug babe

This doodlebug babe was born with aplomb
Fair blown out of bed by a flying bomb.
But wait - can first memories ever be true?
I can't remember. I haven't a clue.
All is recalled from a fog filled haze
There was no YouTube in those distant days.
Just hordes of buzz bombs that spoiled our fun
And rained on Raynes Park: but what had we done?
The church up the road was razed to the ground
We raced to see, it was fun being around
No thought of the danger that stalked our lives
No sense of risk from a bomb that arrives
Dropping its calling card with eerie noise
Before the engine cuts out thrilling us boys
Then mother shouted as we jerkily felt her
Dragging us into the Anderson shelter,
Praying in vain that the bombs would away
So we could go out to resume our play.

The War

Looking back, the War was not what it seemed;
Memory blurs the real from the dreamed.
Now I mostly recall bits in between:
Mum herding us to the ham and beef shop
Sheltering us from objects about to drop,
We didn't think to ask her why
No need to make a hue and cry.
I can still smell intoxicating smoke
In those smouldering furnaces of coke
From steam engines at King's Cross
As we travelled to Bradford all at a loss

They gave it a name, evacuation
Clearly, some civil servant's creation
We stayed with Uncle Nicholas, but not for long.
It was soon obvious something was wrong.
Relatives had their own private war
And that was the last of our cousins we saw.
We moved to a place we called nanny goat land
(Thus nostalgia for country life was fanned)
Near a school where we slept most of the day
With the stench of cabbage never far away.
The rest of the war?
Just the odd punctuated sound
Destined in memory to resound
A siren filling the air with rage.
We didn't understand, those of our age,
And still don't
Or won't
Though we are said to have turned a new page.

Austerity

A period of austerity followed the War:
I know, I read it recently in a book.
But we never knew what we never saw;
What's not there doesn't get a second look.
We kids, well, we just had a life to live.
We didn't figure that a low life spiv
Was selling nylons in short supply;
As a boy it hardly caught the eye.
To us the commodities most royal
Were condensed milk and cod liver oil.
We thought it was bliss and it still is
But better not say, you know how it is.
In days of plenty whatever they say
It's uncool to like war-time food, you may
Be deprived of a packet of cigs
Or put on a diet of syrup of figs.
Then came liberation and the New Look
Though we still saw life through the ration book;
Nothing spoke more of war's futility
Than everyone's clothes being strictly Utility.
Today everyone competes for different clothes
At least in theory, but fashion fiends
Usually end up wearing torn jeans.
Maybe Utility has triumphed, who knows?

School daze

The war had stopped when school came to pass
Yet some of the kids brought grenades into class
That they'd found on a dump.
But nothing interrupted
The unexploded silence of the classroom.
We, forty pupils never spoke, unless asked,
Fear is indivisible
Especially after a war.

Cigarette cards

The pride of my youth, the peak of my fun
Was collecting cigarette cards, one by one:
A child's glimpse of an adult's world
As the wonderful captions were slowly unfurled,
Committed to memory as if by rote
Like "Craven A will not affect your throat",
Or "Flow gently Sweet Afton among thy green brays".
Each label, we never doubted, does what it says:
Gold Leaf, Capstan and Woodbine
(though of honeysuckle born
Would later on become a word of scorn)
I didn't know then that the ciggies I saw
Would kill more folk than the Second World War.

Marbles

Forget your leap frog and your hop scotch
Or "O'Grady Says Do This". For me
One game only was top-notch:
Marbles, played for all to see
On open land, and in its way,
The Grand Theft Auto of its day,
Fought in mean streets with real fights
As homespun rules were banged to rights.
Our marbles went on a suburban ride
Out in the open with nowhere to hide.
Funsies, Keepsies, Lardee we screamed
As we played out our war, or so it seemed,
And rolled out our balls of coloured glass
Oblivious to what might come to pass.
The friendships lost best remain unsaid
As we battled to keep our street-won cred.
Now games have left the streets to be on screen
But don't say progress.
Think what might have been.
Modern games have not got better,
Just lost their marbles.

Scrumping

We loved scrumping.
Great windfall of youth
It wasn't just the act -but what was heard:
The thumping sound of the word itself
So, let's go scrumping, scrum-ping:
Not stealing, not thieving, just scrumping.
Robbing, as everyone knows, is a crime
But scrumping means rescuing apples in time
Before they rot or decompose
Like a discarded rose
That's beginning to fade.
It had all the thrills of a commando raid
Over the wall and among the trees,
In and out in two minutes. What a breeze.
Beautiful Bramleys and oh richest prize
Cox's Orange Pippin, try them for size.
That was the king of the apple tree
A Garden of Eden moment for me,
A time to savour and feast and sing
Not robbing, not thieving, just scrumping.

Phoney

I can remember the first time the telephone rang,
I was fourteen years of age.
It was newly installed
In a corner of the hall awkwardly walled
Off from the rest of the flat,
In case it did something unexpected -
Like ring.
Which it did after a week,
It could have awakened the dead.
It was a friend who had called
Because someone had said
We'd had a telephone installed.
Now, over 50 years later
It is still in the hall though now fixed to the wall
And, once again, it doesn't ring at all.
We keep it though, we phone-o-philes
It's company for the nearby mobiles.

Sweeping Roads

On the broom
I remember it well
Brush, brush,
forward, forward
always forward
Push, push
take a breather
grab the shovel
push, push
to and fro
don't look up, just down
you in the middle of town
expelled from school
(Never mind - breaking some rule)
totally invisible to passers by
(When did you last speak to a road sweeper or even try?)
yet curiously at peace in you own anonymity
a parallel planet where silence is
your guardian angel.

The thought occasionally occurred
one could be immersed in this pleasant strife
for all the rest of one's working life
It is difficult to escape present horizons
Some things are better looking back
Nostalgia paints a fairer picture
But there was always going to be a price
To be locked in a day dreamer's paradise.

Losing class

Somewhere along the line -
Between the end of rationing
And the Suez Crisis - I lost it.
Not my innocence *(later, later)*
But something
Equally irretrievable,
Once gone.
My class
(You don't seriously mean irretrievable, do you?)
I am still searching for a clue:
Was it passing the eleven plus?
Maybe it was grammar school
(You didn't have to go)
That sucked me into its
Oh, you know, its middleclassness
(You are making it sound predestined)
Or was it my accent slowly but surely
Adapting to those around it
(You could have resisted, but you didn't, did you?)
Maybe it was my perceptions of others' perceptions of me
(My, we are getting philosophical)
Why can't all writers call themselves working class?
You can't have working class writers, it's true
If the act of doing it disqualifies you.
Truth is I never left the working class
(Ha, ha, kiss my arse).

First estate

Even an estate agent would be pushed for words
To describe where we lived but let's have a try:

"Constructed on a historic site, handy for road and rail
And no need to move when you reach old age".

That was true in its way
though you could also say:

"Ghetto built on the site of a scarlet fever hospital
Overlooking the main road to London
With the main railway line to the left,
While to the right and behind,
Oh make merry, such a sight,
The tick-tock allure of a cemetery".

Politicians sure knew how to stack life's race
And keep the working class in their place.

Raynes Park

Everyone has a Raynes Park
in the suburbs of their minds,
somewhere to go as life gets hard,
a bottomless pool of childhood bliss,
where all was good that could be good,
apple trees, bikes, recreation grounds,
scrumping, laughing and paper rounds
the sound of birds that sang unseen
and green the most imagined sheen
on drip-dried afternoons that had no end
For all that was bad is lost in time
and the need to survive.
Everyone needs a Raynes Park
though they may not call it that
Ours was a special one. It's still there
when we need it most
and have nowhere else to go.

Skips

Skips, barometer of urban living,
are for unwanted sinks,
sofas, socks
discarded clocks,
torn kites broken bikes
yesterday's Nikes
To be cleared away
To make space for tomorrow.
I'd like to dump memories in that skip
then I can start again
without stockholded pain
They'll be gone by morning
moved without warning.
I hope some passer by
will find them a good home.

Funeral

Funerals are where the living die
and the dead meet up
in the shrouded silence of unfamiliarity
"What a shame we only have craick
on occasions like this,"
said Auntie Agnes turning her back
while cousin Jane tries in vain
to remember my name.
Always prefer the playing field of the dead
to the cemetery of the living.

Underground

Blind black man on the Underground,
Appearing out of the blue without a sound
Except for your white stick tap tap tapping.
How did you get here, into this compartment,
And what am I supposed to do
Since no-one is getting off at Waterloo?
I hold your arm, see you onto the platform,
Shout for help: "Could someone kindly
Take this gentleman to the escalator!".
Someone does, just as the door closes
And shuts me off.
Now you are gone, I suddenly
Want to know more:
Where have you come from
What did you bring that Argos bag for?
What happened in your life till now
And what will happen hereafter?
Suddenly, too late, I,
A blind white man, want to know.

Nun on a train

She was quite short in the main
In a habit of dark blue
This nun on the train
Who boarded at Waterloo.
But I had to refrain.
I had too much to do
To ask her
Where she was going,
Did she have doubts,
Was she always right,
What did she read,
Did her thoughts wander
In bed at night,
This nun I nearly met on the train.
At the next stop she was up and out of sight
With a sort of a hint of a smile
At me, then was lost in the rain,
This nun I nearly met on the train.

Summer

Summer came tardy one day
Licking the rooftops dry
Pulling the vegetables high
There huddling away
Playing hide and seek
with the sky.

Ground under

What is it about a packed train
That makes chatty folk from speech refrain
The nearer you are to someone's cheek
The less likely you are to speak

Face in the Crowd

He picked her out
Unknowingly
(Or did she pick him?)
As he was going up the escalator
And she going down
A Face in the Crowd
Their eyes met
Momentarily
Laser-locked in a mesh
For a fraction of a second
As if one flesh
But the escalators moved on
Eye contact gone
He up
She down
End of a story
That never began.

Brickbats, a painted poem

(Carl Andre's bricks installation at Tate Modern)

In the view of some well known critics
it's a spiritual/material balance
a "harmony of proportion and order"
To others - just a load of old bricks

I had a dream last night
I entered Tate Modern, albeit half tight
and exchanged the bricks for replicas. Right.
Now, is it the same work of art
if Andre himself can't tell them apart?

Maybe the art doesn't just depend
on particular bricks end to end
What counts is the concept and not the parts
if you want to score points in performance arts
Now what I want to know from you
is this. Fast forward 10 years hence
No one will have noticed unless I'm dense
So, pray, tell me what's its true fate
Is the real "Andre" at home by my grate
or lying in state at the Modern Tate
Or have I in the fullness of Time
stumbled upon a victimless crime?

Tate Modern (1)

Making electricity
Carsten Holler's Unilever installation featured children's slides in the Turbine Hall of Tate Modern (October 2006)

Pity those paintings you see on the wall
No match for these slides in the Turbine Hall
Where people are flocking to see them all
Backwards and forwards like a shopping mall
Sometimes from above it looks like a den
Or a Lowry scene with those matchstick men
Or a giant tank in Damien's name
Putting people, not sharks, in the frame.
At other times it has a cathedral charm
Only running children breaking the calm.
This is a gallery where people are the art
Not visiting but acting out a part.
Art stays put on the walls, no longer the king
It watches from afar this new found thing.
In truth, the Turbine Hall generates more
electricity now than in days of yore.

Tate Modern (2)

Whose fault?

Doris Salcedo's "Shibboleth" at Tate Modern (2007) - a curving crack the length of the Turbine Hall

The tectonic plates shifted slightly
Overnight.
Now you must decide
Which side of the divide your feelings reside.
Yes, take sides.
Yesterday it was no more
Than just another turbine floor.
Today it generates a rift,
A grand canyon of the mind
Creating a seismic shift,
Between those that laud a work of art,
And those not able to tell it apart,
Who see no more than a flaw on the floor.
What does it mean this seismic scene?
East versus West,
Rich versus poor,
Mod versus trad,
The crack in our minds?
Or a gap in which art is trapped,
Its intended fate
To be two sides of a debate.
If you can't decide which to back
At least have a good crack.
Meanwhile, children scamper, unaware
Of the real meaning of the tear.
There's nothing puts the critics on attack
More than children and artists having craic
But life, you may think, is bit like that:
Not easy to tell the craic from the crack.

Graffiti Grove

(near Waterloo station)

For art like this you need no optician
It's in your face, instant cognition
Graffiti is art without permission
And there's no greater treasure trove
Than Waterloo Station's Graffiti Grove
A bit of London set apart
For wild daubs and urban art
But wait, my friend, what's happening here
Should fill street artists with mortal fear
For when such work has official sanction
Its funeral rites are as good as done
Guerilla art is no longer plied
Official endorsement is suicide

A wrecked car at the Imperial War Museum

(A Jeremy Deller installation)

It's only a car
Not worth a look
In a junk yard
One more mangled motor
Rust ridden
Plateless
Marque not clear
Owner unknown except
Dead
Killed by a suicide bomber
With 38 others
100 injured
Including five sons of a café owner
News for a day
March the fifth 2007
In Bagdad
In the book market
East of the Tigris
On al-Mutanabbi Street
Named after a great Arab poet
Who believed in books
But was murdered
With his son.
A poem of his had given offence
Over a thousand years ago
In 965.
Death still inhabits the street
And this car
It will never leave
God is good
God is good

Lines written on Lambeth Bridge

From Lambeth Bridge if you look downstream,
The might of England jostles to be seen.
Leftwards, the force of law through Parliament
On the right, Lambeth Palace from Heaven sent.
Both powerful buildings that do not beauty lack
But on which wordy Wordsworth turned his back.
Not so the other William - Blake - who lived nearby
And saw the town with an unblemished eye.
In the slums of Lambeth where he would go
Seeing no joy but marks of weakness, marks of woe
In the faces he passed by in the street,
Or wandering whores he chanced to meet,
In his agony of morning, silent, bare
Earth had not anything to show less fair.

Hardy's Tree

(An ash tree in St Pancras churchyard where Thomas Hardy maybe waits for his wife)

There's a Fraxinus excelsior in the churchyard of St Pancras
A hardy perennial, it's Hardy's tree, an Ash.
Dating from 1865 when Hardy was partly in charge
Of the Midland Railway's plan to enlarge
The railway at the expense of the old churchyard.
He had to do it though the task was hard
And the tombstones he moved, he put by a tree,
Which, enveloped by roots, are still there to see,
Conjuring up memories which when unfurled
Give us a glimpse into Hardy's darkling world
Stand there. Stay still. Bury that fear.
Do you not feel his hauntings here?
When failing light has departed into night
And poems put the madding crowds to flight.
Yes, he hovers around this Ash, with its octopus roots
Gripping the tombstones so,
not letting death go,
Like clips from a Stanley Spencer apocalypse.
His wife, ashen, waiting in turn
for her loved one's return
To a place she knows he goes
Where he gathered these tombstones long ago
And left them by this tree for a rendezvous
Of true souls separated only by death.

Stand-up Poet

Oh, rare Ben Jonson,
As should be known
by every London cabbie,
He lies buried standing up
In Westminster Abbey.

Creedo

(Martin Creed, the minimalist artist at Tate Britain)

Martin Creed has won more fame of late
With humans sprinting up and down the Tate.
It's the new world of modern art
Everyone can run their part.
His BlueTac on a wall was also art;
Tacky it's not, it has given him a part
In the Pantheon of the greats of modern art.
His most famous work, also at the Tate,
Was a room with a light going off then on.
Ignorant folk thought he was taking the rise
Not this lad, it won him the Turner Prize.
He should have won a Green award I plead
Because if everyone followed his Creed
It would halve the voltage we need to exist
And make every homeowner a modern artist.

Damien Hirst's Pharmacy

I suddenly became sick
At the Saatchi gallery on London's South Bank,
(you know, the one with the shark in the tank).
Unfortunately, I took ill
(overcome by the thrill?)
While admiring Damien's Pharmacy,
A masterpiece of medicines on shelves
And rows and rows of pills
An installation for all ills.
I only wanted one.
"It might save my life," I said.
"Sorry," said the curator:
"It's a Work of Art,
the whole depends on the part.
Art is indivisible".
"But one won't be missed.
Think", I gasped,
"Art or Life which comes first?"
"Sorry," he said, "you'll have to ask Mr Hirst."

Still life

(Mistaken for a masterpiece)

Duane Hanson is not what he sounds like
(a pensioned-off guitarist from the sixties).
but an artist making eerily life-like sculptures
of ordinary people, bag ladies to booksellers,
sitting around strutting their stuff.
London's avant garde Saatchi gallery,
Which aims to shock, purchased
a number and spread them around
an exhibition where they frequently scared
first-timers who thought they were real
(and burglars at night).
So, there I was,
staring at a large canvass
in a quiet room in the gallery
entitled "Rave".
I was motionless as I
tried to take it all in.
Then I must have moved
and a woman passing by
jumped in shock
thinking a sculpture had come to life.
It is difficult to explain the feeling
of momentarily being a work of art:
It's like a religious experience.
That moment will always exist,
shared by two people from afar
who don't know who each other are:
bonded by a moment in time
when art concealed art.

On trying to paint Lucien Freud

(from a photo)

Lucien Freud
Always annoyed
Depicting a void
Those eyes,
Their size
Those lies
Looking not at you
but through you
to the mess inside
humanity that died
As the Freudian slip
Tightens its grip.

London lights

London is not light
But light is London.
In the unwarming morning
Light pierces the buildings
With sideways swipes.
In the evening the sun drops,
Stealing the light from the fading glow
Snatching the city back.

Underground poem

I've always wanted to write a Poem on the Underground
Every artist needs a platform
But I don't fancy extolling Bakerloo
hardly a romantic thing to do
If I left it on the Northern Line
the rats would eat it rhyme by rhyme
And the Jubilee would be
too much of an extravaganza
for my modest, unscheduled stanza
But I must do something or my poem will rust
unpublished never to age in use
or be victim of a critic's abuse
Never mind if it doesn't rhyme
as long as it gets there on time
But I must be published first
so to put it in circulation
I'm leaving this verse of mine on the Circle Line
where it will go round and round
until it is found.

St James's Park

(By the lake)

Londoners no longer need
Their lust for country life to feed
For nowadays most country life
Retreats to town for our delight.
The fox was first to try this stunt
It came to town to flee the hunt.
But now you're in St James Park
And half the farmyard's at this lark:
The geese that in the country snap
Will eat stale bread straight out of your lap.
Now squirrels from your fingers feed
And seagulls swoop for all they need.
Daft ducks won't let you pass until
From your bare hands they eat their fill,
As pigeons on your shoulders land
And pelicans might brush your hand
As tame as cats for all to see.
So, welcome to the town . . . country.

Mulberry Fair

(A Mulberry Tree on crutches in St James Park)

Let's hear it for the mulberry.
The bush that wants to be a tree.
Nothing wrong with high ambition
Unless you start from a weak position.
The mulberry found a false solution
To fight the force of evolution.
The fact is, as all can see
It was never meant to be a tree.
Have you ever seen one without support
All its growth hormones come to nought?
Instead of leaning on steel girders
To keep it in a state unbended
It should remain as Nature intended:
A simple bush that can be danced around:
"Round and round the mulberry tree";
Doesn't read like poetry to me.
Mulberry, mulberry,
Take it from me
You were never meant
To be a tree.

Mulled berry

(On the proposed destruction of two mulberry trees in Temple Gardens, London, 1998)

Walking to work in Temple Garden
where flowers bloom and barristers harden
passing the planes and false acacia
I was shocked by a note pinned to a tree
a sentence of death for the mulberry
accused of 'affecting the area'
as though they had caught malaria.
Yet these lovely old trees
do only please
their one crime is not having the power
to charge 200 pounds an hour
like the rest of this shower
I think that we should the Bar remind
that mulberry made Silks for their kind
and with such love for the past
to let these trees breathe their last
Sooner the Silks be locked in the Fleet
Leaving justice and life to the mulberry.

The Longest Garden

Let's praise London's secret fact
The jungle by the railway track
A garden unfolding as your carriage moves
The burden of the day it subtly soothes
Blackberries unpicked and elderflowers
That calm the weight of passing hours
Ash, oak and fledgling trees
Catch the eye with flashing ease
Convolvulus, the brute, is also there
All plants on its rampage soon to ensnare
And what's that whizzing past my eyes
Could it be Berberis with butterflies
While Rose bay willow drooping in the rain
Flutters in the wind of our speeding train
We know this land should have better uses
(Build more houses. No excuses)
But until then while politicians harden
Inhale the bliss of London's lost garden.

London Plane

Does the city deserve you, London Plane
spectacular in everything but name
whose roots Romans watered with wine
endowing them with powers divine
and returning Greeks gave arms
in recognition of your balms
under whose dappled, protective branches
Hippocrates taught medical advances.
Today Platanus' survival wheeze
is to do a seasonal strip tease,
shedding surplus bark with ease.
If that were followed by other trees
Plane wouldn't be London's main species.
Sweet Plane, ignored lung of the city's lair,
breathing and filtering our polluted air
why do we still need to be reminded,
walking blindly, that you are still there.?
Perhaps we should elect you arboreal mayor.

But wait! Before you bend too far to please
this tree is no more the Council's solution
Local treasurers are now discarding
the plane and planting the Chinese ginkgo
There's less cost for care and no pollarding
For ginkgos survived the ice age and snow
The plane's fate is no longer a mystery
Its job is done.
Gratitude belongs to history.

Verses in praise of the (English) discoverer of "Champagne"

(Christopher Merret who is buried in St Andrew's Church, Holborn)

What makes Champagne go full throttle
Is secondary fermentation in a bottle
This is an invention without which
Sparkling wine would be mere kitsch
And who made this spectacular advance?
Why, in folk law, a monk, Dom Perignon of France
But wait: hear Christopher Merret's scientific view
Which he wrote in sixteen hundred and sixty two
Without any mock Gallic piety
He told the newly formed Royal Society
He'd discovered this spectacular advance
That let wine ferment in bottles first
That were strong enough not to burst
T'was Britain's gift to an ungrateful France -
Decades before they gave sparkling a glance
It created that country's strongest brand.
So, let's raise a glass in our hand
To a great man's invention from afar
And drink to the Methode - not Champenoise
But what it should have been called; Merretoise.
So, let all by their merrets be
Judged that the whole world can see
That however we may be thought insane
We gave the French - for free - Champagne.

Chateau Tooting

Fine wine, we are authoritatively told
Must be fondly nurtured before it's sold
Canes carefully pruned, from classic vines
All trellised out in tight battalion lines
And picked on the best day of the year.
These are rules to which you must adhere
If you want to make a drinkable wine
Or else your efforts will wither on the vine.

Which is what makes it all so cool
That Chateau Tooting shatters every rule
Grapes are drawn from gardens and allotments small
Or maybe hanging from a neighbour's wall
From the extremes of London near and far
Though no one knows what vines they are

And all brought to a central pick-up place
On a given time and so starts the race
To get the fruit to a winery fast
Where using skills quite unsurpassed
Their alchemists turn this base London mould
Once a year into viniferous gold
Which is why I am usually rooting
For South London's prime wine, Chateau Tooting.

Visiting a relation

It was Spring once more and I thought it good
To visit a relation if I could
And the one I would mostly like to see
Was one who never yet has talked to me

I found him quite soon on the internet
Who shared my genes though we'd never met
Yes, lots of data about my near relation
And easy to find their exact location

I set off with satnav to chart my course
Bussing and walking to my stated source
Till my satnav said with smug elation:
"You have now arrived at your destination"
And there he was my nearest relation
With whom I shared a genetic connection
Of ninety-nine per cent of my DNA
But now I have met him what should I say?
I look at him and am quite impressed
Except perhaps by the way he is dressed
He's got eyes and nose and feet and legs
And yet his appearance a question begs
For though genetically he's just like me
I'd better admit . . . he's a chimpanzee

I wonder when he looks at me so sage
Why is it him not me locked in a cage
Being gawped at by all at London Zoo
I have to admit, I haven't a clue
For looking at him it's plain to see
But for a genetic slip he could be me

Perhaps, he thinks in his mind it's been shown
It's me behind bars and him free at home.

There could be a lesson to be unfurled
As you read about wars all over the world
Maybe, this is the moral that works out the best
We fare better with chimps than most of the rest.

City slickers

How vainly men their lives extend
To build vast wealth they cannot spend
Which if they did, such spending power
Would boost the economy hour by hour
Instead all choose the same way to relax
They phone their accountant to pay less tax
And in order to make their conscience free
They turn it into a philosophy
And choose a word in French - yes, Laissez-Faire
Hoping the blinded workers will not care
So the rest of the world their wealth may see
All, please you, won by armchair industry.

Underground

A young woman stood up without a sound
In a crowded carriage on the Underground
I thought she was leaving at the next station
Till she looked at me puzzled for a short duration
Then smiled and pointed at her vacant seat
I knew I should have conceded defeat
She was rightly doing what she'd been told
Though she was telling me I was too old
To be left to stand on my own two feet
I should have said Yes and embraced defeat

But too quickly I thanked her and politely said No
Not thinking that this might be such a blow
She may never do such a good turn again
I tried to explain but it was all in vain
She had sunk back into her book
Not deigning to give me another look
Her mum had told her to help the elderly
But that training had failed for all to see
So an old man could keep his punctured pride
And try to keep standing for the rest of the ride.

In Praise of GI Joe

How many people, these days, will know
The tale of a pigeon called GI Joe
The least likely hero ever to show
Truth is he didn't himself even know

He flew 20 miles from a battle zone
Where there was no workable telephone
Across the fields at 60 miles an hour
The greatest example of pigeon power
To say that the allies had captured a village
So there was no more need to bomb or pillage
Pigeon post said Vecchia had been taken
And the planned bombing would be mistaken
It was an act that saved a thousand lives
And a village that might have died survives
There were lots of similar pigeon tales
Go look up the books and see the details
Though what they need is not a tutorial
But something in stone, a true memorial.
Trafalgar Square is the obvious place
There already exists there a vacant base

But wait
It's not so easy to fix their fate
Pigeons in fact are banned from the Square
It's only for national heroes says the Mayor
Who has declared the Square a no-go area
For pigeons whose presence creates hysteria
These birds they claim are nothing but vermin
Statues near Nelson must show their ermine
Men like Havelock and General Napier

Skilled at war and handy with the rapier

But don't forget the unsung heroes of war
A vital part of our military corps
Who saved thousands of lives with secret flights
Unknowingly saving our human rights
They gave the Dicken Medal to GI Joe
The only bird to be honoured so
For bravery that saved a thousand lives
But little of whose memory now survives
Let's hear it for Joe and his pigeon friends
For years of neglect let's now make amends
Where are the politicians who will act with verve
To give these pigeons the plinth they so deserve.

On the statue of Sir Henry Havelock

(in Trafalgar Square)

I suppose an apology would be in order
(You were obviously used to orders)
I have passed you by almost daily without really looking,
Except at the inscription
which says "Erected by public subscription."
Which I presumed needed the usual political decryption
And really meant erected by public conscription.
But apparently not.
I researched further and found
You were a fellow of universal renown.
Pubs, streets and towns the world over
Are named after you.
Crowds mourned your death,
You were a national hero, a celebrity of your day,
After your campaigns to suppress the Indian affray
(Though over there they might not have seen it that way).
You have one other claim I should mention,
A bit of trivia that might raise a smug laugh:
Your statue's the first carved from a photograph.
Which I will remember as I snap to attention
When I'm next in the square, camera-phone in hand,
Passing you by en route to the Strand.

Nelson's column

(A true story)

A middle class woman on a 24 bus
surrounded by children all in a rush,
middle class all
with accents that pall,
they stretch their necks
from the upper decks
observing the sights
as they speed along,
they quietly greet
Victoria Street
and stare
at Parliament Square
unmoved in Whitehall by Number 10
they hit Trafalgar Square
and then she proudly says:
"This in the middle is Nelson's column."
"Oooh," they cry together, suddenly enthused:
"Nelson Mandela!"
"No," says the woman unamused
her voice fading as she speaks
their attention now unwrapped
She trying to recover her brain
"It was, er, oh, it doesn't matter:
just an old English sea captain."

Trafalgar Square

Bless you Trafalgar, you are not so Square
When you think of the history buried there
Nothing around you is as it might seem
Even "Trafalgar" will fail as a theme
Tourists they come from miles to stare
Yet Nelson was never meant to be there
Charles Barry, the architect, wanted to see
The middle of the square reserved to be
A place for the new Royal Academy
A companion for the National Gallery
But a committee of Parliament resisted
And with an eye on history insisted
That a column for Nelson be forthwith built
Even though the King's reputation might wilt
For the name was changed as you may be aware
From 'William the Fourth' to 'Trafalgar Square'
Poor King William, spare him a thought
The monarch whose glory came to nought
He not only lost his square but, truth to tell
He lost his memorial statue as well
They couldn't raise money enough for his plinth
And it has stayed there empty ever since
It's currently home to a rotating sculpture
Which defines such modern art as culture
From which Nelson on a column so high
Doubtless can turn a haughty blind eye.

I remember London

I was born in low rise London
Which has now all but gone
In those balmy days buildings knew their place
Before planning became an endless race
They were intended to be no more,
Than the height of the buildings right next door.
Centre Point produced the first pain
We never thought they'd do it again
Monstrously, it was built a la mode
Destroying the lines of Tottenham Court Road
Built to appease the emerging Gods fiscal
It became not a one-off but a starting pistol
For a race to the sky by developers all
Determined to profit from urban sprawl
Of all the buildings in London the most tall
For centuries was the Fishmongers Hall
Built close by London Bridge to the north
But look now at the concrete that has poured forth
Fishmongers' Hall is now a mere mound
Dwarfed by giant new buildings all around
Have we nothing to show more fair to our Creator
Than a Gherkin, a Walkie Talkie and a Cheese Grater?

City Fair

London thou art a city fair
(It's true for we have it from the Mayor)
Tourists come because the city rocks
If they can see it through the office blocks

Necropolis Railway

The Necropolis Railway at Waterloo
Conveyed dead people no matter who
From a station in London's centre, no joking
To a fresh built city for the dead in Woking
No probs as long as you paid for a pass
Which could be first, second, or even third class
As in life, so in death, you must know your place
As well as being in a state of grace.

The most famous customer so history tells
Was Communist founder Frederick Engels
Whose principles should have - oh let it pass
What does it matter if he travelled first class
You don't want dead bodies to lose any face
When you're gone, class distinction leaves no trace.

On arrival at Brookwood, there's a religious test
One station for Protestants and a second for the rest
(Remember - even when you bury your dead,
There's a risk that a religious virus could spread)
So, let's give thanks to the railway of Necropolis
For helping God sort bodies before the Apocalypse.

Shard

Still
Don't
Know
Whether
To like you,
Or hate you.
Too soon yet
To tell I guess.
Like unsought
Liaisons it takes
Time to gel. You
Have invaded my
Personal space, you
Have now shattered
The silence of the sky,
Stalking me wherever I
Walk. Each glimpse I get
Of the city has to include
You; always looking down
On me like a godly chaperone
Even when my back be turned.
Who can tell what future giants
Will follow this precedent you've
Set. Intruders all–I doubt it will ever
Stop now our defences are truly down.

Plaque on the wall

It's not a column, nor statue, it's true
It could be grey but it's usually blue,
It's just a plaque on an outside wall.
You could fix your own on a wall in the hall.
But sadly it won't be the same you see,
For it needs the seal of the right committee
Which thinks you are someone above the norm,
Whose name on a plaque won't generate scorn.
But there's another reason you should dread
For to get a plaque you have to be dead.
So, until that happens go forth, walk tall
Rejoice that there's no writing on the wall.

St Mary's Woolnoth

This unreal church would never have been here
If planners were allowed to get too near.
For it was standing blithely in the way
Of the City and South London Railway
Which planned to pull it down to build the Tube at Bank
And all the local opposition to outflank
Yes, Hawksmoor's masterpiece was found
To be in the way of the new Underground
The Tube had got planning permission
In the eighteen nineties for demolition
To turn this building from heaven to hell
To show the church for whom tolls the bell
But this feisty church didn't do submission
Parishioners declared total opposition
Until Mammon did a compromise devise
To preserve the church suitably re-equipped
while extending the station into the crypt
And there the story ends except for a postscript

You may feel that this church in sacred space
If nothing else must be blessed with grace
And so it was because in earlier times
Its pastor in truth had been soiled with crimes
He had been a slave driver on the high seas
Till a vision from God brought him to his knees
And raised him from this position so base
To be a priest and write a hymn: Amazing Grace.

City Churches

Stop thinking of them as churches
Built to worship something up there,
Think of them as urban sculptures,
fantasies in stone,
a rich landscape of public art
unchanged for hundreds of years
except for the surface damage of the elements.
Now dare to dream
that the office blocks between them
will suddenly disappear,
leaving a churchscape of Hawksmoors and Wrens.
leaving us to ponder how so much beauty
could be produced in adoration
of something that may but may not exist,
often by artists who didn't believe.

Mausoleum of Madness

(The Imperial War Museum)

Pause your step as you walk through the door
Into the Mausoleum of the whores of war.
Our whores for sure but whores just the same
Whose aim, like theirs, was to kill or maim.
Visitors rarely have time to consider
It's just Death's hardware sold to the highest bidder.
But this Museum of Madness has a story visitors can find
Which evolved from madness of a different kind.
On this site notorious Bedlam stood,
The original mad house where people could
Pay a penny and gawp at the inmates
Chained to their cells and confined to their fates.
Treated insanely when needing attention
Which prompts one more thing needing a mention,
Bedlam still exists in a leafy part of Kent
To which mentally ill patients are sent,
To seek and receive world class treatment.
Such progress as this one could never resent,
But when Bedlam left this building we find
It sadly left the madness behind
When it shut its last door.
If we had made such progress in war
As we have made in the field of mental health
What peace there would be with such new found wealth.

London Underground

An announcement from London Underground
to our valued customers:
Mind the gap Mind the gap
Would customers please
Mind the gap.
Mind the gap
Mind the gap.

An announcement from valued customers
to London Underground:

Mind the gap,
Mind the gap?
Mend the ****ing gap

City

London You are no simple City
Showing off to please the few
Travellers passing through.
You have to be found
Sought, hiding underground
Beneath floors
Behind closed doors
Stalking alleys off the street
Buried under layers deep.
Rivers lost for generations
Still water your foundations,
Churches suffering a belief rupture
Are now revered as public sculpture.
Everything in London ever built
Is still there under clay or silt,
The dead of London
Still haunt us there
In some form, underneath.
London is built on bones
Decomposed dust
And crushed buildings,
Like a layered cake
The past builds the present,
Won't let go.
Drill down and you will find
History's mystery may not be kind.
This city is a giant recycling machine
To the present generation unseen,
Only memories are left intact
Passed on by generations past.
Walk carefully, not so fast

The past is in you burned
A lesson that has to be learned.
Respect these walls or you will rue
Times ahead for they will devour you too.
No structure gone requires our pity
In this God's own embalmed city,
Which no longer has a deity to see
But still radiates its own infinity.

The Widow's Son

(Poem in praise of The Widows Son pub, Bromley-by-Bow)

The widow's son who died at sea
That others in this land be free.
Lingers in a pub in Bromley-by-Bow
Where every year the world should know
The memory of this boy lives on
Though hope of seeing him is now long gone
He never returned from Napoleon's war
But in case he did his mother swore
A hot cross bun to leave by the door
Which has happened each Good Friday since
When Navy chums this custom do evince
Adding a hot cross bun with East End feeling
To a net that falls, hauntingly, from the ceiling
A grave of buns just like a hanging mast
Bringing memories of Good Fridays past
Whose memories in this net are here interred.

Unclubbable

He read the obituary with pride and joy,
Tracing his father's life since he was a boy.
Most of the achievements were pleasant to see
The writing, the giving, the OBE,
Except at the end where it simply said
"Blackballed from the Garrick".
That's worse than dead.
He wondered who'd made such a decision,
To subject the family to everlasting derision,
Making him simply "unclubbable".
That's what they do when the prisons are full,
But gaol has an end, it's not like Hell.
Mr Unclubbable is a leper with a bell
Warning other club members to keep away,
Now it's too late for him to have his say
Many are chosen but few are called
He's now withered, deceased
And, worse than that: blackballed.

To Margate without...

We did something crazy before too late
Walking from London to distant Margate
We opted to start in Trafalgar Square
The centre of the capital from where
Close by the statue of King Charles mounted
All distances from London are counted
Doubtless he's thinking of how he was led
Down Whitehall to where they cut off his head
But we must be brave - we must not lose ours
Nor our feet if it's in our earthly powers
For our only rule was an adopted code
We were not permitted to cross a road
Yes, that was our bold, self-inflicted fate
Without leaving the kerb to get to Margate
The route from Nelson was near at hand
It was under ground and into the Strand
Where you can imagine our elation
On finding a subway into the station
But then we were both at a bit of a loss
Where the hell do we go from Charing Cross?
On the walkway above old Villiers Street
It was starting to look we might have to cheat
If we were to avoid ignoble defeat
Then we stumbled across one of London's gems
For Hungerford Bridge goes across the Thames
And the Embankment - to The Thames south bank
Where it is fitting to pause here to thank
The planners - was it planned? - for all their wiles
Made it easy to walk for miles and miles
Along the river without crossing a road
Or encountering any transport mode
Because, and pause for this moment of elation,
There's near total pedestrianisation
What other capital city in the world
Has at its heart such riches unfurled?

So, once over Hungerford Bridge, turn left
And walk to Tower Bridge of worries bereft
Past restaurants, galleries and theatres bold
Which a modern Wordsworth could have extolled
Turn left at Tower Bridge past City Hall
And when it seems you're riding for a fall
You find underground steps to Katharine's Dock
Your bumptious critics thus to mock
And then, oh Father Thames, this is so rich
By hugging your banks we get to Greenwich
Where genius engineers were able to deliver

An underground route to cross the river
From the north bank at Island Gardens Park
To the jewel of Greenwich, the Cutty Sark
There turn left with detours where necessary
To that walkers' heaven the Thames estuary
There is the occasional deviation
By housing estates of man's creation
But none will breach your conduct's code
As long as you avoid crossing a road
Which we did as we headed towards the sea
Sorry, that was a slip. Did I say "We"?
The fair weather walkers answered their muses
And one by one they made their excuses
And left me alone to hang on my fate
To walk by myself to the sands of Margate
Which I did over a period of weeks
Straining to the limit my walking techniques.

If you deem this a fantasy of mine
Go try it yourself and drop me a line...

Londoner

I am London, boy and man
As long as you don't dare to scan
My lineage now so widely spread
That Britain's history can be read
Among the genes of forebears dead
Foreigners who left their lairs
To make by conquest, England theirs
Picts, Romans, Saxons and Nords
Who left the beauty of the ffords
To ravage England's land so fair
Before them hunters from God knows where
Later Jews, Huguenots, Italians, believe me
Flooded London from across the sea
Without whom there'd be no growth in GDP.

Power

We all rule powerfully
In the empire of our minds

Sweet Thames

Sweet Thames run softly till you get a shock
When your flow is blocked at Teddington Lock,
As the gates close, it's the last sanctuary
Against the tidal flow from the Thames Estuary.
When the gates open your course is resumed
But you must steep yourself to be consumed
By the upcoming surge that's not your fault
It's alien water and full of salt

Your waters soon will the saline offend
But not till you flow past Battersea's bend
No longer that Thames of which I sing
Bringing fresh water from a mountain spring

You now feel the sea of mystic powers
Backwards and forwards every few hours
Rising by several meters and then down
As dreary commuters sleepwalk through town.

The Two Thames

(History of a river)

This is a tale of two rivers which look the same
But which have nothing in common except a name
Thames West starts in the hills and flows along
And gently it will till I end my song
Through nature's curves and man-made weirs
Through meadows fair till London town it nears
Past Runnymead, Kingston and Hampton Court
Much history it has watched, seen battles fought
Leaving memories of rural bliss unfurled
God's in his heaven, all's right with the world.

UNTIL: until it meets a rival beast
A fearsome foe they call Thames East
Which has massed its forces wherever necessary
From the North Sea to the Thames Estuary
Now, it launches its attack wave after wave
Making Thames West its conquered slave
It roars past Tilbury, Gravesend, Rotherhithe
Forcing Thames West to retreat with each tide
Its flow to the coast thus forced to abate
Never reaching the sea in its pristine state
The closest fresh water gets, experts agree,
Is the bend to the river around Battersea
From there to Gravesend there's a brackish mix
As when salty brine to fresh water sticks
From then the Thames no longer walks so tall
It's no longer a real river at all.

Thames sonnet

(after George Turberville's The Lover to the Thames of London)

A mongrel stream with often moody tides
In Cotswold hills from silken springs does rise
Creeping through meadows where the cowslip hides
Near drooping trees that cramp your flowing sides.
Flow sweetly till the furious sea you meet
Will stain your pristine flow with brackish look
And hurl you back upstream in forced retreat
Mix salt into the sweetness of your brook.
While you whose watery wars do thus prevail
Splitting the town in two from north to south.
Londoners know themselves from where they hail
As can be heard from every open mouth.
But they all know what lies behind each squall
Without a Thames there'd be no town at all.

Thames Estuary

Walking along the Thames Estuary
You feel the city is running out of breath
And a strange dream begets
As the river ever wider gets
Houses and factories become sparser
Mud gets thicker, the water murkier
Reeds reedier as they shed the townscape
As a river slowly becomes a sea
With the tide changing quite soon
In the morning and afternoon
Though where this happens
Is beyond my observation
All you see is civilisation
Ebbing out to sea
And the soft mud on the river bank
Trapping the funereal detritus
Not something that claims renown
Except for someone escaping
The claustrophobia of the town

Plagiarism

Plagiarism should be a capital offence
(It's mainly done in the Capital)
Until Time starts revealing
Those actually good at stealing
Shakespeare being the most cool
The exception always proves the rule.

Lundenwic

We learn of ancient Greece and Rome
But not of history nearer home
If in time travel I had wandered down
To live my life in Lundenwic town
There'd be no one but Saxons there
From Fleet Street to Trafalgar Square.

Canute

(If this incident happened it likely took place in the Palace of Westminster by the tidal Thames.)

Great King Canute once sat along the shore
With all his doting courtiers spread before,
All waiting for a move from him
The power of the waves to dim,
To prove to them that this King's might
Bestowed on him, a divine right.
But instead of making the waves surrender
Canny Canute had another agenda.
He wanted to show to his subjects all,
They were wrong to hold him in such thrall:
He was no miracle worker at all.
So, sat on his throne by the water side,
He yelled "Stop" to the incoming tide
Which, unlike his subjects, ignored his plea
And flooded the sands with a rising sea
Which kept on rising for hours and hours
Thus undermining his Kingly powers.
Canute emerged a lesser king
But a better man. And one final thing:
The moral of this, which may seem unkind,
Is that miracles are mainly in the mind.
It won't stop the false tale of King Canute
being re-run with yet more fibs en route
To uproot a myth from the common lore
Would need a real miracle, that's for sure.

Walbrook River

They called you "brook", not a river at all
Since you skirted one side of London Wall
Hailing from Curtain Road in fair Shoreditch
Where holy monks a priory did pitch
In Holywell where Shakespeare's first plays
Were staged, the population to amaze.
You emerged from a spring and wormed your way,
Around watchful churches through mounds of silt
To where the Bank of England later was built
From there another gracious turn you took
Passed Hawksmoor church, St Stephen's Walbrook,
And soon after the statue of Mithras, you meet
Then you burst into the Thames near Cannon Street
These days you get neither sight nor sound
From the Walbrook now buried deep underground
Its course by history has been suppressed
Of all London's lost rivers, this is the lostest.

Tourist walking down the Mall

As he was walking down the Mall
He thought he saw a pedestal
But as he gradually got nearer
And the mist lifted, becoming clearer
He saw something more grand and solemn
A large soldier standing on a huge column
And he thought to himself a little wryly
He must be special to be thought so highly
But what it was he couldn't fathom
That merits being stood so high up a column
And was he surprised by all the local talk
That they had erected it for the Duke of York
Who in Georgian times caused comic relief
By being so bad a commander-in-chief
Leading the whole country a dance
By losing wars in Holland and France
Marching men to the top of the hill in great pain
Only to march them down again
People in those days laid satiric bets
That he was put on a column to escape his debts.

The Albion Works

In its day it was a wonder of the industrial world
When a plant milling flour around the clock unfurled
Central London's brazen solution
To being left behind in the industrial revolution
Positioned south of the Thames by Blackfriars Bridge
It belched forth smoke and fumes in deadening profusion
Triggering deep local opposition to a landscape defaced
From people and local millers whose jobs were displaced
But it was a local resident, William Blake who had had his fill
And described it to posterity as a "dark satanic mill"
Metropolitan critics presumed henceforth
That dark satanic mills should be in the north
But the smoke and pollution that then burst forth
Was not up there but down here at Lambeth north.

On the occasion of Unilever's sponsorship of Hamlet for the Royal Shakespeare Company in December, 1992

Squeegee, or not Squeegee: that is the detergent:
Whether t'is nobler in the mind to suffer
The slings and arrows of outrageous dentures,
Or to take Gibbs against a jaw of troubles,
And by some brushing end them? To dye, to bleach?:
Omo; and with some Surf to say we end
The heartache and the thousand natural stains
That cloth is heir to. Oxo is a consomme
Devoutly to be wish'd, To sup, to slurp;
Persil to stain: ay, there's the rub;
For in that slurp of mouth what dirt may come

When we have shuffled off this mortal coil,
Must give us Pears. There's the respect
That makes Eternity of so long life;
For who would bear the whips and scoops of Wall's
Obsession's odour, the proud man's Cornetto,
The pangs of dispriz'd Lux, Lifebuoy's decay,
The insolence of butter, and the spurns
That patient merit of the unworthy takes,
When he himself might his Fray Bentos make
With a bare Boursin? Who would fardels bear
To grunt and sweat under a weary life,
But that the dread of something after death,
The undiscovered armpit from whose stench
E'en Calvin Klein recoils, puzzles the till,
And makes us rather bear those ills we have
Than fly to others that we know not of?
Thus conscience doth sell Impulse to us all;

And thus the native hue of resolution
Is sicklied o'er with the pale cast of thought,
And enterprises of great Unilever
With this regard their profits turn aright,
And lose the name of action. Soft you now!
Elizabeth Arden! Nymph, in this Bird's Eye
Be All my Vims remember'd.

My new guardian angel

I'm no longer alone with no one to care
now I know that you are there
following me everywhere
I sense you always close to me
wherever I am you can see
your contact is quite discreet
following me down the street
switching to a colleague
when your eyes show fatigue
Though I know you not
you know me a lot
(I hope you won't tell
of last Wednesday in the doorway:
I didn't know her well)
Time, I suppose, will tell
You are my guardian angel
looking over my shoulder
always with eyes on me
my ubiquitous, loveable CCTV.

London ambulance

The ambulance goes speeding by
Super duper
(if you belong to Bupa)
It races past Westminster Hospital,
now luxury flats, anxious not to be last
then past St Georges Hospital
(now a swanky hotel) carrying its load
to Cromwell Road
to a marvellous new hospital
medical nectar
for the private sector
The ambulance flies past sporting an elegant green stripe
leaving me with one small gripe:
Will it deign to stop for me
if I can't afford its fee?

London Commuters

(Faces on the Tube)

Death masks,
Sullen,
Unalive,
Hanging from straps,
Bodies attached
Like meat in an abattoir.
Dead souls undone
Struggling voiceless through unlife
Hidden behind newspapers,
their daily shrouds,
or buried in books
or these days, a Kindle.
Later, decanted from carriages,
sucked like zombies into
mausoleums unseen
where work reluctantly takes place,
They suddenly come alive
by the coffee machine:
Daily proof
of the resurrection
of the dead.

Concorde's Last Flight Over The Capital

Supersonic stud
seen but no longer heard
You broke the sound barrier
the class barrier
the fashion barrier
But sadly not the cash barrier.
When they finally towed you to rest
two decades after your birth,
you became
yesterday's plane.
Yet to us, you will always look
like something
designed for tomorrow
awaiting recall.

In praise of curries

Mainly eaten in London

Softly, the saffron scent subsides
As cardamon its odour throws
And coriander fights with mace
Sending fierce opiates behind my face,
Unleashing juices in a race.
Cumin, ginger and tumeric combust
Spontaneously inside my mouth
Ignited by the thought of chilly.
All this sitting at home in a flurry
Just thinking about ordering a curry.

Serpentine Red

(After seeing Jean Roupel's all red pavilion at the Serpentine Gallery)

Just suppose, the world's all red,
Just so, a monochromatic rainbow
Tables, chairs, walls, floors,
Red, red, red, would give us pause.
We'd still have sunsets, I suppose
Variegations of red on rose
Lighting up a ruddy sea.
Traffic lights would change from puce to red,
And then to rose to let you move ahead.
Red leaves teased from magenta trees
Flutter down their scarlet trunks.
The skills we put into projecting colours
Would be equally cool it must be said,
Painting a million shades of red.
For red is a great leveller
No colour prejudice, not even in the mind,
Unless it be a prejudice of hues
Which is progress of a kind.
You'd have all the joy you'd ever need
Just be careful not to bleed.

London Banker

"So what will you be doing next, your life to fill?"
(asked the professor of his graduating pupil).
"I want to extract millions from savers
without scruple,
By exploiting the law at every loophole
And milking the taxpayer
without bothering to thank her.
And to make it a little more craven
I'll hide the takings in a distant tax haven."

"Thank God," said the mentor.
Who couldn't speak franker
"At last, I've tutored an honest banker."

London walker

Slow down.
Sell the car.
Get off the bus
UnBoris the bike.
Hit the ground walking
Be led.
Down alleys,
around corners,
along canals
Through churches
let the buildings do the stalking

Stop staring at those passing faces
on a conveyor belt to God knows where.
Don't walk the streets
Let them walk you
Duck the straight line of the road ahead,
the linear prison of the motorist's eye
Walk, walk, up, down, around town,
don't ask why.
Here, there, stop,
gawk,
turn,
inhale,
take pride
Let the nooks and crannies be your guide
Unlock the history that cities always hide
in townscaped mystery
From uncurious commuters they can't abide.

Ageing in the capital

You are finally old in London, I'm told
When an unseen curtain comes down for certain
And people no longer ask for your age

They just look at you, see signs of life's knocks
And quietly tick Senior Citizen in a box
Before letting you through at a special price
Which I suppose in its way is really quite nice
For it removes the fear
That someone near might hear.
After all you can't help growing old
But you can stop others from being told.

John Ball

When Adam delved and Eve span,
Who was then the gentleman?"
Where are you now, mighty John Ball
When poor people need you most of all
To spell out in a simple rhyme
The defining madness of our time
Once Eden fairly shared the common wealth
But now the Rich have stolen it by stealth
Grabbing to themselves the lion's share
Of all the wealth accountants can ensnare
Convincing the poor it will trickle down soon
And pigs will fly to the Man in the Moon

John Ball tried his homespun solution
Simply said, it was Revolution
But the Peasants' Revolt was cruelly put down
In Smithfield square in London town
When The King reneged on his pledge to reform
And unleashed in revenge a murderous storm
John Ball was killed and quartered by the King
But his words live on with a contemporary ring

Printed in Great
Britain
by Amazon